# Your first 100 words in FRENCH

## French for Total Beginners Through Puzzles and Games

*Series concept*
Jane Wightwick

*Illustrations*
Mahmoud Gaafar

*French edition*
Teresa Braunwalder

*McGraw-Hill*

Chicago  New York  San Francisco  Lisbon  London  Madrid  Mexico City
Milan  New Delhi  San Juan  Seoul  Singapore  Sydney  Toronto

Copyright © 2002 by Gaafar & Wightwick. All rights reserved. Printed in the United States of America. Except as permitted under the United States Copyright Act of 1976, no part of this publication may be reproduced or distributed in any form or by any means, or stored in a database or retrieval system, without the prior written permission of the publisher.

3 4 5 6 7 8 9 10 11 12 13 14 15 16 17 18 19 20 21 22 23   VLP/VLP   0 9 8 7 6

ISBN 0-07-139599-7
Library of Congress Control Number: 2004053059

Cover design by Nick Panos

McGraw-Hill books are available at special quantity discounts to use as premiums and sales promotions, or for use in corporate training programs. For more information, please write to the Director of Special Sales, Professional Publishing, McGraw-Hill, Two Penn Plaza, New York, NY 10121-2298. Or contact your local bookstore.

**Other titles in this series:**

*Your First 100 Words in Arabic*
*Your First 100 Words in Chinese*
*Your First 100 Words in German*
*Your First 100 Words in Greek*
*Your First 100 Words in Hebrew*
*Your First 100 Words in Italian*
*Your First 100 Words in Japanese*
*Your First 100 Words in Korean*
*Your First 100 Words in Pashto*
*Your First 100 Words in Russian*
*Your First 100 Words in Spanish*

This book is printed on acid-free paper.

# ◎ CONTENTS

# ☺ HOW TO USE THIS BOOK

In this activity book you'll find 100 key French words and phrases. All of the activities are designed specifically for developing confidence in the early stages of learning a language. Many of the activities are inspired by the kind of games used to teach children to read their own language: flashcards, matching games, memory games, joining exercises, anagrams, etc. This is not only a more effective method of learning new words, but also much more fun.

We've included an **Introduction** to get you started. This is a friendly introduction to French pronunciation and spelling that will give you tips on how to say and memorize the words.

Then you can move on to the 8 **Topics**. Each topic presents essential words with pictures to help memorization. There is a pronunciation guide so you know how to say each word. These words are also featured in the tear-out **Flashcard** section at the back of the book. When you've mastered the words, you can go on to try the activities and games for that topic.

Finally, there's a **Round-up** section to review all your new words and the **Answers** to all the activities to check yourself.

Follow this 4-step plan for maximum success:

**1** Have a look at the key topic words with their pictures. Then tear out the flashcards and shuffle them. Put them French side up. Try to say the word and remember what it means. Then turn the card over to check with the English.

**2** Put the cards English side up and try to say the French word. Try the cards again each day both ways around. (When you can remember a card for 7 days in a row, you can file it!)

**3** Try out the activities and games for each topic. This will reinforce your recognition of the key words.

**4** After you have covered all the topics, you can try the activities in the Round-up section to test your knowledge of all the French words in the book. You can also try shuffling all the 100 flashcards together to see how many you can remember.

This flexible and fun way of learning your first words in French should give you a head start whether you're studying at home or in a group.

# ◎ INTRODUCTION

The purpose of this section is to introduce the basic principles of how French is written and pronounced. If you understand these principles, you will have a head start when it comes to learning your first words. Concentrate on the main points. The details will come as you progress.

Have a quick look at this section and try to produce the sounds out loud, in a confident manner and then move on to the topics for some practice. As you work your way through the words in this activity book, you will find the spelling and pronunciation gradually start to come more naturally.

## ◎ Pronunciation tips

Many French letters are pronounced in a similar way to their English equivalents, but here are some differences to watch out for. It is these differences that trip up the beginner so try to look over this list and say the words out loud using the pronunciation guide.

| | |
|---|---|
| **r** | a French **r** is produced from the back of the throat; imagine that you are gargling, e.g. **robe** *rob* (dress) |
| **ch** | like *sh* in "shirt," e.g. **chaise** *shaiz* (chair) |
| **j, g** before **e** or **i** | a French **j** or soft **g** is pronounced like the *s* in "pleasure," and is written as *zh* in the pronunciation guide, e.g. **jupe** *zhewp* (skirt); **boulangerie** *booloñ-zhayree* (baker) |
| **i** | like *ee* as in "feet," e.g. **divan** *deevoñ* (sofa) |
| **au** | like *o* as in "over," e.g. **chaussure** *shoh-sewr* (shoe) |
| **eu** | like *ur* as in "fur," e.g. **fleur** *flur* (flower) |
| **oi** | like *wa* in "wax," e.g. **poisson** *pwassoñ* (fish) |
| **ou** | like *oo* in "poor," e.g. **bonjour** *boñzhoor* (hello) |
| **ui** | like *wee* in "sweet," e.g. **cuisinière** *cweezeen-yehr* (stove) |
| **er, ez** (at end of word) | like *ay* in "play," e.g. **nez** *nay* (nose) |

## ◎ Silent letters

French has many silent letters.

**h** is always silent, e.g. **hôtel**, pronounced *ohtel*.

Many other silent letters fall at the end of words. Watch out in particular for the silent final **t**, **d** and **s**:

**lit** (bed), pronounced *lee*

**canard** (duck), pronounced *canar*

**dos** (back), pronounced *doh*

The pronunciation of Louis (*loowee*) Armstrong is a good example of the French silent final **s**.

✔ Many French letters are pronounced the same as English, but some need special attention

✔ **h** is silent, as are **t**, **d**, and **s** at the end of words

## Accents

The French language has four accents which can influence pronunciation. Three of these are written above a vowel:

´ written above an **e** as in **vélo** *vayloh* (bicycle)

` also written above an **e** as in **étagère** *aytazhair* (shelf)

^ written above any vowel as in **âne** *ahn* (donkey)

The fourth accent is a little squiggle below the **c** (**ç**), pronounced as *s* as in **français** *froñsay* (French).

## Nasal vowels

Nasal vowels are a vowel and an **n** (**an**, **en**, **in**, **on**, **un**). They are pronounced in a similar way to the English *ng* as in "go*ng*" or "e*ng*age" but said through the nose and mouth at the same time.

The nasal vowels give French its distinctive character; it sometimes helps to pretend to have a cold and speak with a "congested nose."

In the pronunciation guide for the 100 words, the nasal vowels are written with *ñ*:

| pants | **pantalon** | *poñtaloñ* |
| stomach | **ventre** | *voñtr* |
| rabbit | **lapin** | *lapeñ* |
| hello | **bonjour** | *boñzhoor* |

# Stress

In English, the first syllable of a word is usually emphasized or said slightly louder than the rest of the word (<u>fac</u>tory, <u>win</u>dow, <u>rab</u>bit). The French pronounce each syllable with equal stress or degree of loudness, producing a more even sound.

✔ French has four accents: **é, è, ^,** and **ç**
✔ You need to perfect your nasal twang to sound French!
✔ French pronounce words with even stress

# Masculine and feminine

In English, the definite article is always "the," e.g. "the table," "the door," "the river." In French, nouns (naming words like "table," "door," or "river") are either masculine or feminine and the definite article changes accordingly: **le**, pronounced *ler* (without saying the "r") for masculine (**le divan**, "the sofa") or **la** for feminine (**la table**, "the table"). If the noun starts with a vowel or **h**, the definite article is **l'** for both masculine and feminine (**l'ordinateur, l'usine**; "the computer, the factory"). In the plural it is **les**, pronounced *lay*, as in **les cheveux** (literally "the hair<u>s</u>").

It is important as you progress in French to know whether a word is masculine or feminine and, for this reason, we have given the 100 words with their articles. Try to get used to learning new words in this way – it will help you later.

# Similar words

You probably already know more French than you realize. There are many words that are similar to English. If you apply the principles of French spelling and pronunciation in this introduction, you can say them like a local.

Here are some examples of words that are very similar in French and English. With these words and the 100 key words in this book, you will already have made progress more quickly than you imagined possible.

**le taxi**, pronounced the same as the English

**le bus**, pronounced *bews*

**le train**, pronounced *treñ*

**l'hôtel**, pronounced *oh-tel*

**le restaurant**, pronounced *restohroñ*

**le cinéma**, pronounced *seenayma*

**le lion**, pronounced *lee-oñ*

**l'éléphant**, pronounced *aylayfoñ*

**le désert**, pronounced *daysair*

**la télévision**, pronounced *taylay-veezhyoñ*

**le téléphone**, pronounced *taylayfohn*

✔ French nouns are either masculine (**le**) or feminine (**la**)
✔ **le** and **la** change to **l'** if the word starts with a vowel or **h**
✔ There are many words similar in English and French

## ◎ French alphabet

Here is the complete French alphabet with the names of the letters. These can be useful if you need to spell something – your own name for example.

| | | | | | |
|---|---|---|---|---|---|
| A | *ah* | J | *zhee* | S | *ess* |
| B | *bay* | K | *kah* | T | *tay* |
| C | *say* | L | *el* | U | *ew* |
| D | *day* | M | *em* | V | *vay* |
| E | *er* | N | *en* | W | *dooblevay* |
| F | *ef* | O | *oh* | X | *eex* |
| G | *zhay* | P | *pay* | Y | *ee grek* |
| H | *ahsh* | Q | *kew* | Z | *zed* |
| I | *ee* | R | *ehr* | | |

# ① AROUND THE HOME

Look at the pictures of things you might find in a house.
Tear out the flashcards for this topic.
Follow steps 1 and 2 of the plan in the introduction.

### la table
*la tab-ler*

### le tapis
*ler tapee*

### la fenêtre
*la fenetr*

### la chaise
*la shaiz*

### l'ordinateur
*l'ordinatur*

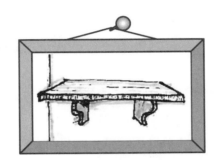

### l'étagère
*l'aytazhair*

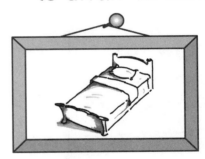

### le divan  *ler deevoñ*

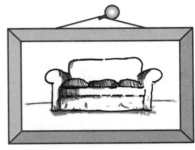

### le lit  *ler lee*

### le frigo
*ler freegoh*

### le placard
*ler plakar*

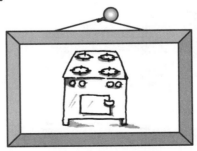

### la cuisinière
*la cweezeen-yair*

### la porte
*la port*

**9**

## ◎ **M**atch the pictures with the words, as in the example.

le divan

le lit

la fenêtre

la table

le tapis

l'ordinateur

l'étagère

la chaise

---

## ◎ **N**ow match the French household words to the English.

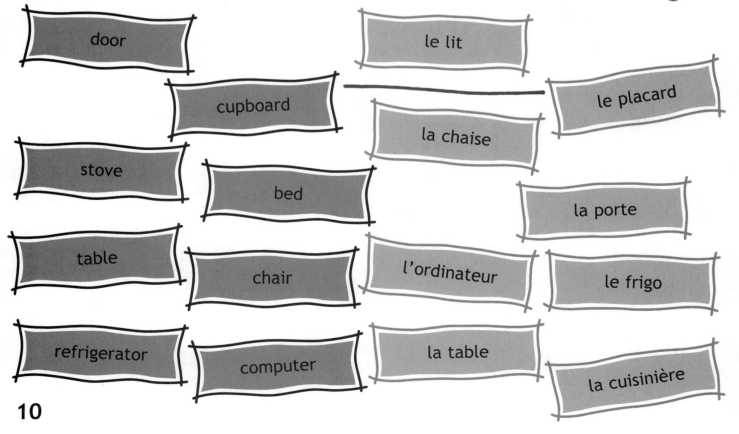

door

cupboard

stove

bed

table

chair

refrigerator

computer

le lit

la chaise

l'ordinateur

la table

le placard

la porte

le frigo

la cuisinière

◎ **F**ill in the missing letters in these household words.

c _ a i _ e        d i _ a _

_ r i _ o        _ l _ c _ r _

f _ n ê _ r _        t _ _ l _

c _ i s i n _ è r _        t _ _ i s

_ o r _ _        é _ _ g è _ _

- - - - - - - - - - - - - - - - - - - - - - - - - - -

◎ **S**ee if you can find these objects in the word square.

The words can run left to right, or top to bottom:

| B | A | T | A | P | I | S | D |
|---|---|---|---|---|---|---|---|
| I | C | U | H | O | R | A | I |
| C | H | L | D | R | V | A | V |
| F | E | N | Ê | T | R | E | A |
| R | L | A | U | E | L | A | N |
| I | R | C | H | A | I | S | E |
| G | D | I | V | A | T | O | E |
| O | E | P | O | R | T | A | T |

11

Decide where the household items should go. Then write the correct number in the picture, as in the example.

1 la table     2 la chaise    3 le divan    4 le tapis

5 l'étagère    6 le lit    7 le placard    8 la cuisinière

9 le frigo    10 l'ordinateur    11 la fenêtre    12 la porte

Choose the French word that matches the picture and fill in the English word at the bottom of the page.

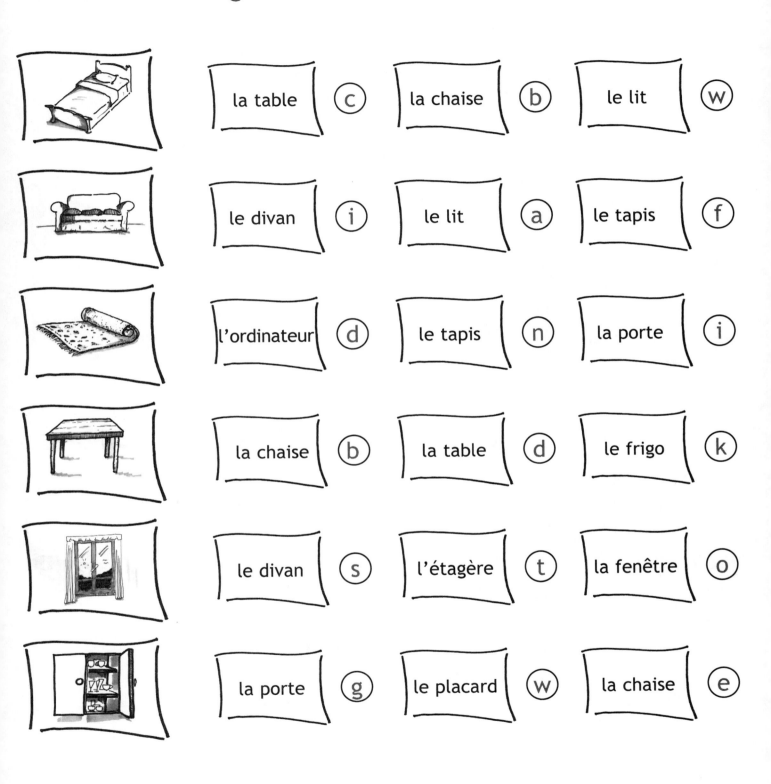

| | | |
|---|---|---|
| la table (c) | la chaise (b) | le lit (w) |
| le divan (i) | le lit (a) | le tapis (f) |
| l'ordinateur (d) | le tapis (n) | la porte (i) |
| la chaise (b) | la table (d) | le frigo (k) |
| le divan (s) | l'étagère (t) | la fenêtre (o) |
| la porte (g) | le placard (w) | la chaise (e) |

English word: (w) ( ) ( ) ( ) ( ) ( )

13

# ② CLOTHES

Look at the pictures of different clothes.
Tear out the flashcards for this topic.
Follow steps 1 and 2 of the plan in the introduction.

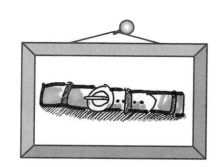

**la ceinture**
*la señtewr*

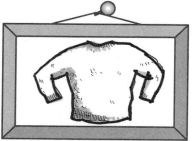

**le pull**
*ler pewl*

**la chaussette**
*la shoh-set*

**la cravate**
*la kravat*

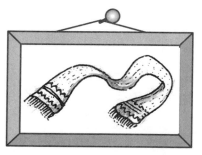

**l'écharpe**
*l'aysharp*

**le pantalon**
*ler poñtaloñ*

**la chaussure**
*la shoh-sewr*

**le manteau**
*ler moñtoh*

**la jupe**
*la zhewp*

**la robe**
*la rob*

**le chapeau**
*ler shapoh*

**la chemise**   *la shmeez*

14

# Unscramble the letters to spell items of clothing.

Write the words with *le, la, les* or *l'*.

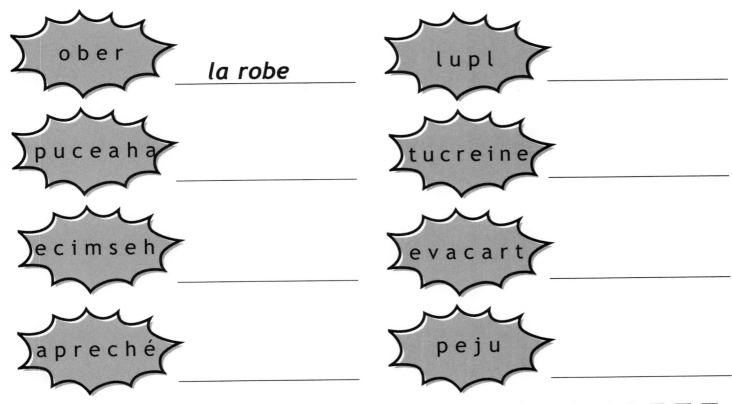

o b e r     *la robe*

p u c e a h a

e c i m s e h

a p r e c h é

l u p l

t u c r e i n e

e v a c a r t

p e j u

- - - - - - - - - - - - - - - - - - - -

# See if you can find these clothes in the word square.

The words can run left to right, or top to bottom:

| F | A | P | C | J | U | P | E |
|---|---|---|---|---|---|---|---|
| I | C | U | H | S | R | A | A |
| C | H | L | E | H | O | N | N |
| J | E | L | M | E | B | T | D |
| A | M | A | N | T | E | A | U |
| P | I | G | S | I | S | L | A |
| C | S | O | U | S | U | O | E |
| H | E | R | A | E | N | N | T |

15

Now match the French words, their pronunciation, and the English meaning, as in the example.

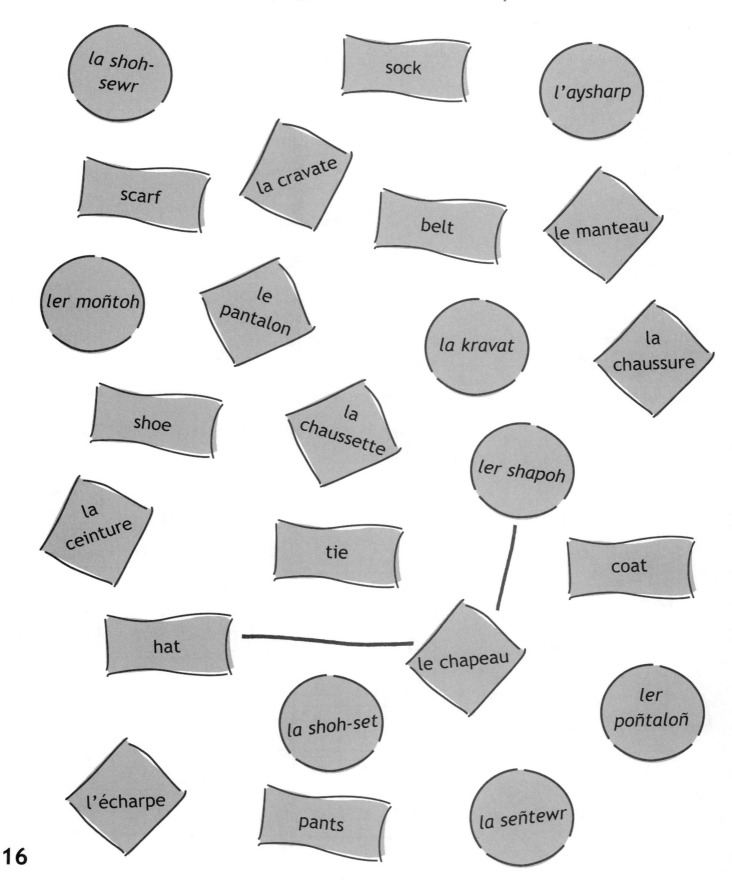

la shoh-sewr

sock

l'aysharp

scarf

la cravate

belt

le manteau

ler moñtoh

le pantalon

la kravat

la chaussure

shoe

la chaussette

ler shapoh

la ceinture

tie

coat

hat

le chapeau

ler poñtaloñ

la shoh-set

l'écharpe

pants

la señtewr

Carl is going on vacation. Count how many of each type of clothing he is packing in his suitcase.

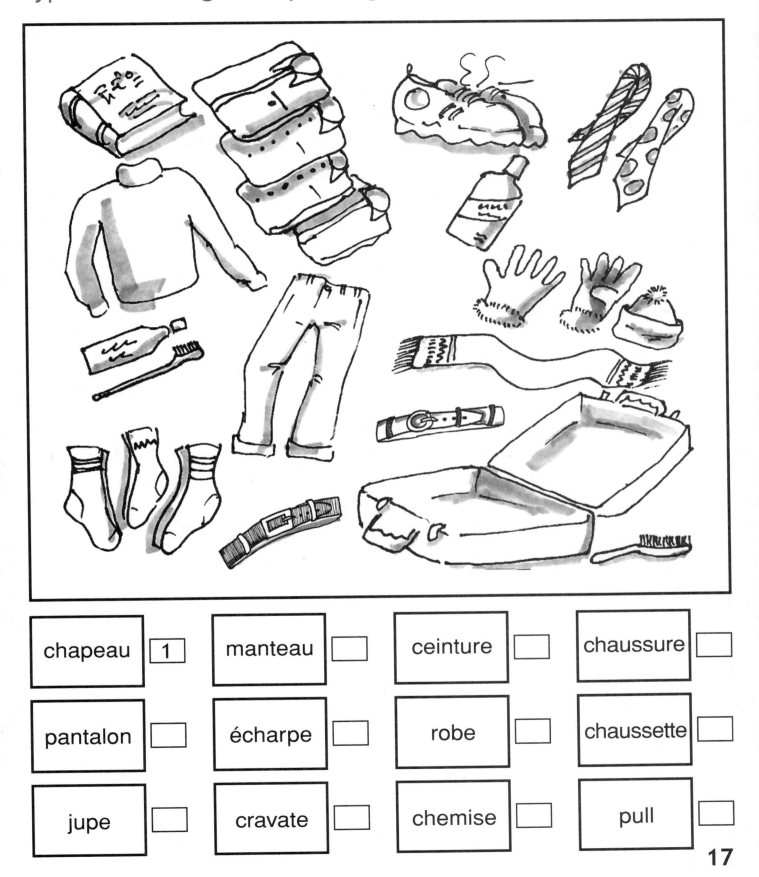

| chapeau | 1 | manteau | | ceinture | | chaussure | |
| pantalon | | écharpe | | robe | | chaussette | |
| jupe | | cravate | | chemise | | pull | |

◎ **S**omeone has ripped up the French words for clothes. Can you join the two halves of the words, as the example?

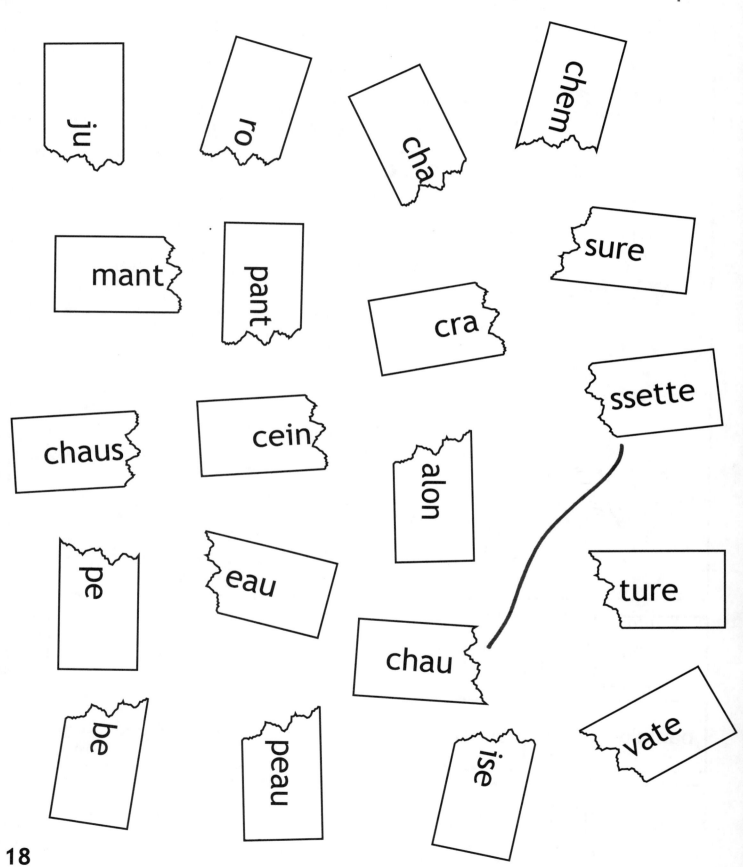

ju

ro

cha

chem

mant

pant

sure

cra

chaus

cein

ssette

alon

pe

eau

ture

chau

be

peau

ise

vate

# ❸ AROUND TOWN

Look at the pictures of things you might find around town.
Tear out the flashcards for this topic.
Follow steps 1 and 2 of the plan in the introduction.

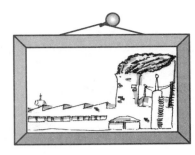

l'usine   *l'ewzeen*

## la boulangerie
*la booloñ-zhayree*

## la maison
*la maizoñ*

## la voiture
*la watewr*

## le camion
*ler camioñ*

## le vélo
*ler vayloh*

## la fontaine
*la foñtain*

## le banc   *ler boñ*

l'école   *l'aykol*

## la rue   *la rew*

le magasin   *ler magazeñ*

## la boucherie
*la booshayree*

## ◎ Match the French words to their English equivalents.

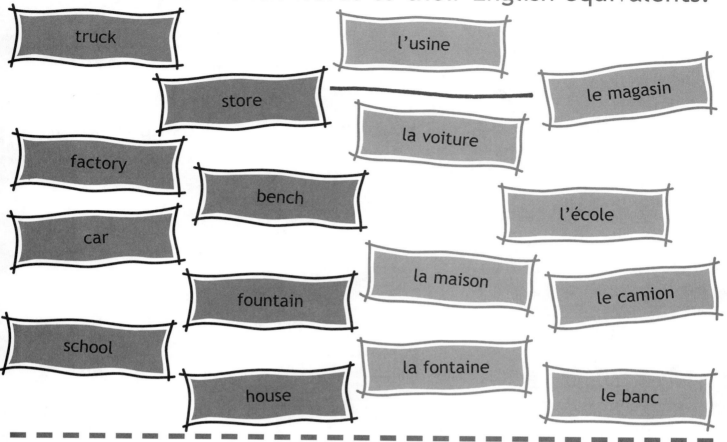

truck

l'usine

store

le magasin

la voiture

factory

bench

car

l'école

fountain

la maison

le camion

school

la fontaine

house

le banc

## ◎ Now put the English words in the same order as the French word chain, as in the example.

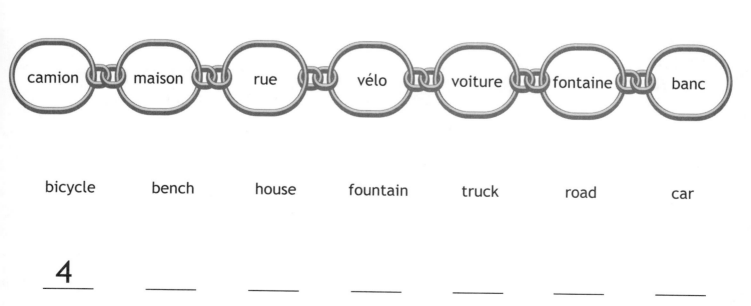

camion — maison — rue — vélo — voiture — fontaine — banc

bicycle    bench    house    fountain    truck    road    car

4 ___  ___  ___  ___  ___  ___

© **L**abel this town plan, as in the example.

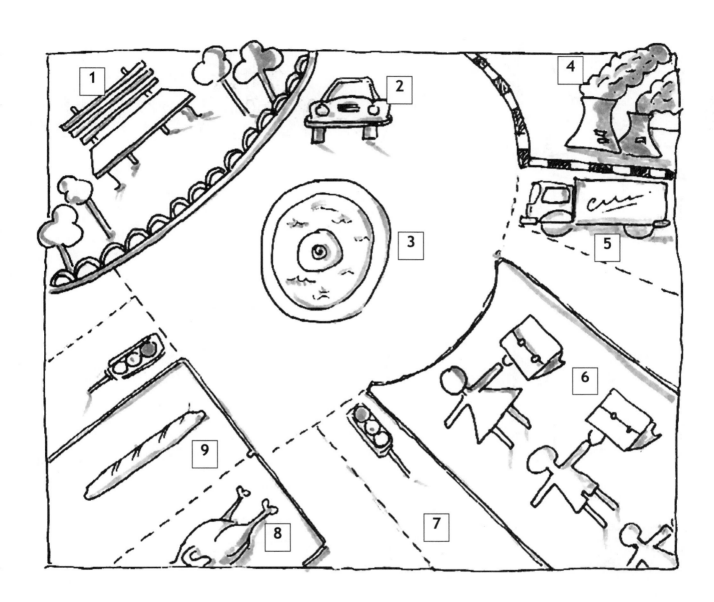

1 *le banc* _____   2 _____   3 _____

4 _____   5 _____   6 _____

7 _____   8 _____   9 _____   **21**

Choose the French word that matches the picture
and fill in the English word at the bottom of the page.

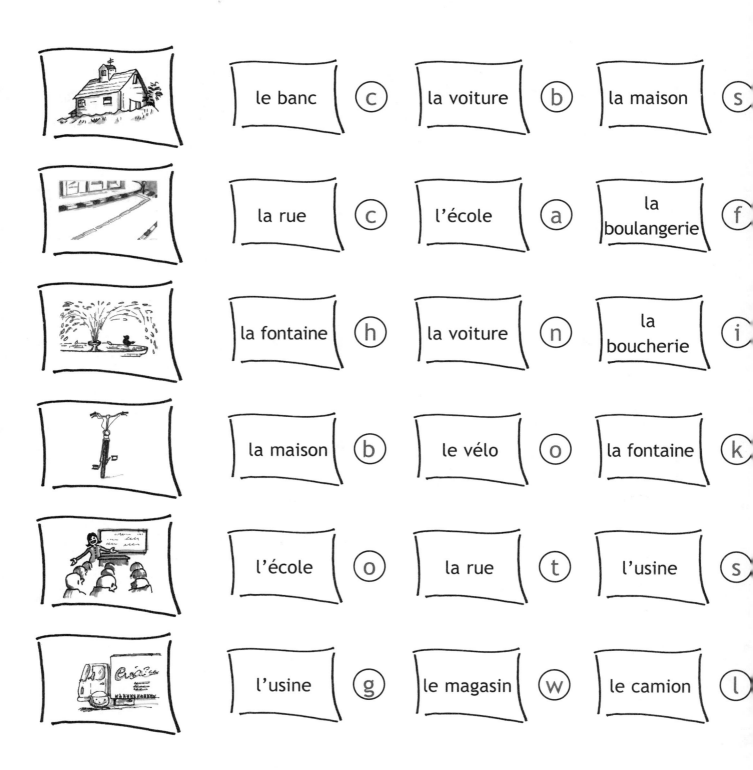

| | | |
|---|---|---|
| le banc ⓒ | la voiture ⓑ | la maison ⓢ |
| la rue ⓒ | l'école ⓐ | la boulangerie ⓕ |
| la fontaine ⓗ | la voiture ⓝ | la boucherie ⓘ |
| la maison ⓑ | le vélo ⓞ | la fontaine ⓚ |
| l'école ⓞ | la rue ⓣ | l'usine ⓢ |
| l'usine ⓖ | le magasin ⓦ | le camion ⓛ |

English word:  ⓢ ◯ ◯ ◯ ◯ ◯

22

Write the words in the correct column, as in the example.

| le | la | l' |
|---|---|---|
| le banc | | |

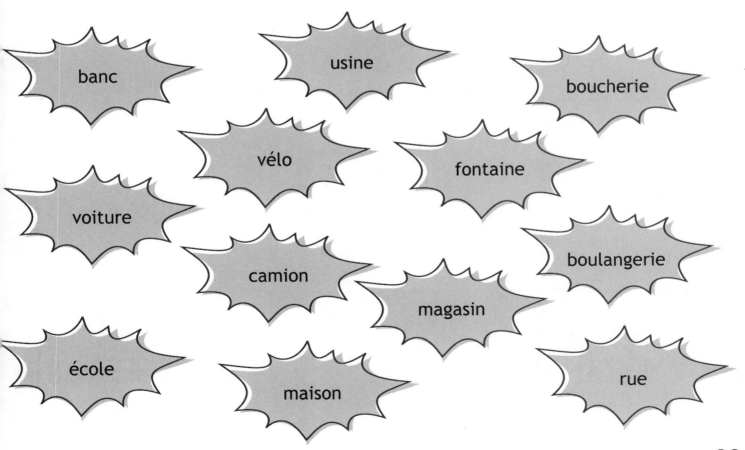

banc

usine

boucherie

vélo

fontaine

voiture

camion

boulangerie

magasin

école

maison

rue

# ❹ COUNTRYSIDE

Look at the pictures of features you might find in the countryside.
Tear out the flashcards for this topic.
Follow steps 1 and 2 of the plan in the introduction.

### la colline
*la coleen*

### le pont
*ler poñ*

### la ferme
*la fairm*

### la montagne
*la moñtanye*

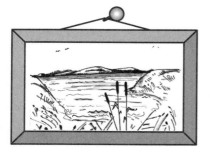

### le lac
*ler lak*

### l'arbre
*l'arbr*

### la rivière   *la reeveeyair*

### la mer   *la mair*

### la fleur
*la flur*

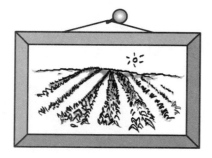

### le champ   *ler shoñ*

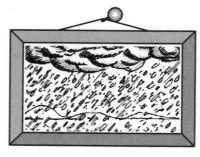

### la pluie
*la plwee*

### la forêt
*la foreh*

24

# Can you match all the countryside words to the pictures.

la montagne

la ferme

la mer

la forêt

la pluie

la colline

le lac

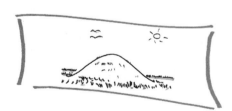

le pont

la rivière

la fleur

l'arbre

le champ

◎ **N**ow check (✔) the features you can find in this landscape.

pont [✔]  arbre [ ]  pluie [ ]  colline [ ]

montagne [ ]  mer [ ]  champ [ ]  forêt [ ]

lac [ ]  rivière [ ]  fleur [ ]  ferme [ ]

## ◎ Unscramble the letters to reveal natural features.

Write the words with *le*, *la* or *l'*.

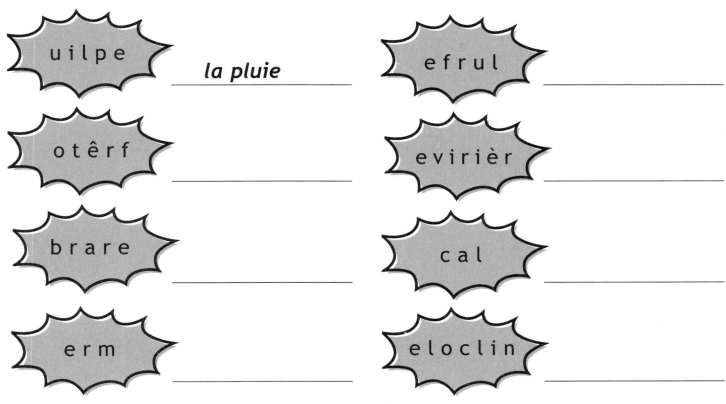

**uilpe**     *la pluie*       **efrul** _____

**otêrf** _____     **evirièr** _____

**brare** _____     **cal** _____

**erm** _____     **eloclin** _____

- - - - - - - - - - - - - - - - - - - - - - - - - -

## ◎ See if you can find 8 countryside words in the square.

The words can run left to right, or top to bottom:

| M | E | P | C | D | A | P | E |
|---|---|---|---|---|---|---|---|
| I | C | C | F | E | R | M | E |
| F | L | E | U | R | B | N | F |
| C | E | L | P | E | R | T | L |
| H | M | F | O | M | E | R | A |
| A | I | I | N | I | S | L | C |
| M | O | N | T | A | G | N | E |
| P | E | E | A | E | N | N | T |

27

Finally, test yourself by joining the French words, their pronunciation, and the English meanings, as in the example.

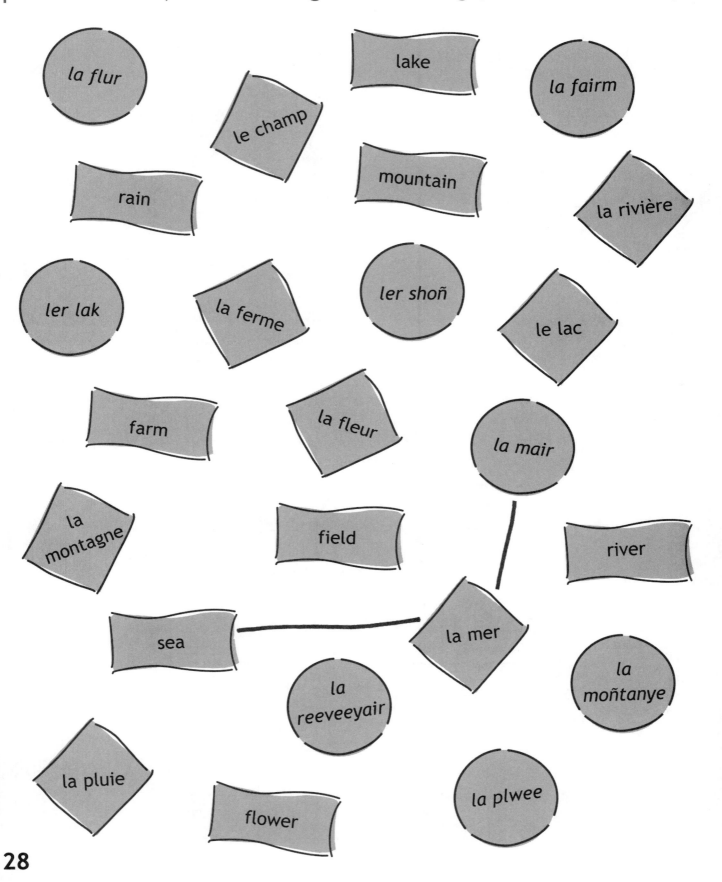

la flur

lake

la fairm

le champ

mountain

la rivière

rain

ler lak

la ferme

ler shoñ

le lac

farm

la fleur

la mair

la montagne

field

river

sea

la mer

la reeveeyair

la moñtanye

la pluie

flower

la plwee

# ⑤ OPPOSITES

Look at the pictures.
Tear out the flashcards for this topic.
Follow steps 1 and 2 of the plan in the introduction.

**sale**
*sal*

**propre**
*propr*

**petit**
*petee*

**grand**
*groñ*

**bon marché**
*boñ marshay*

**léger** *layzhay*

**lent** *loñ*

**cher** *shair*

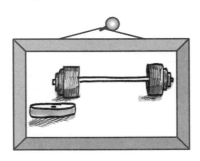

**lourd** *loor*

**rapide** *rapeed*

**vieux** *vee-ur*

**nouveau** *noovoh*

29

# Join the French words to their English equivalents.

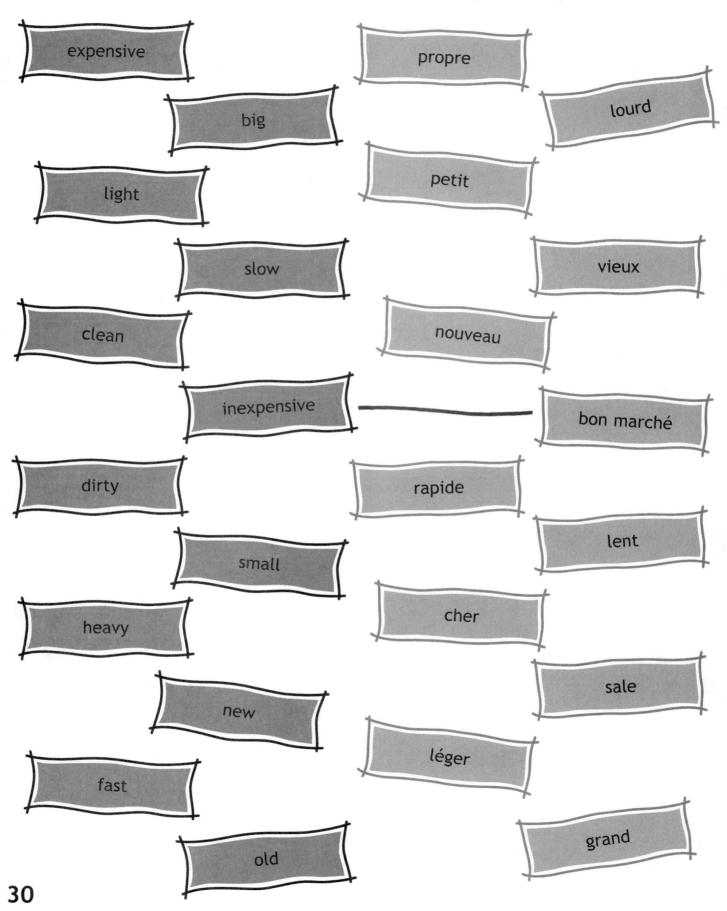

expensive

big

propre

lourd

light

petit

slow

vieux

clean

nouveau

inexpensive ——— bon marché

dirty

rapide

lent

small

heavy

cher

sale

new

léger

fast

old

grand

🌀 **N**ow choose the French word that matches the picture to fill in the English word at the bottom of the page.

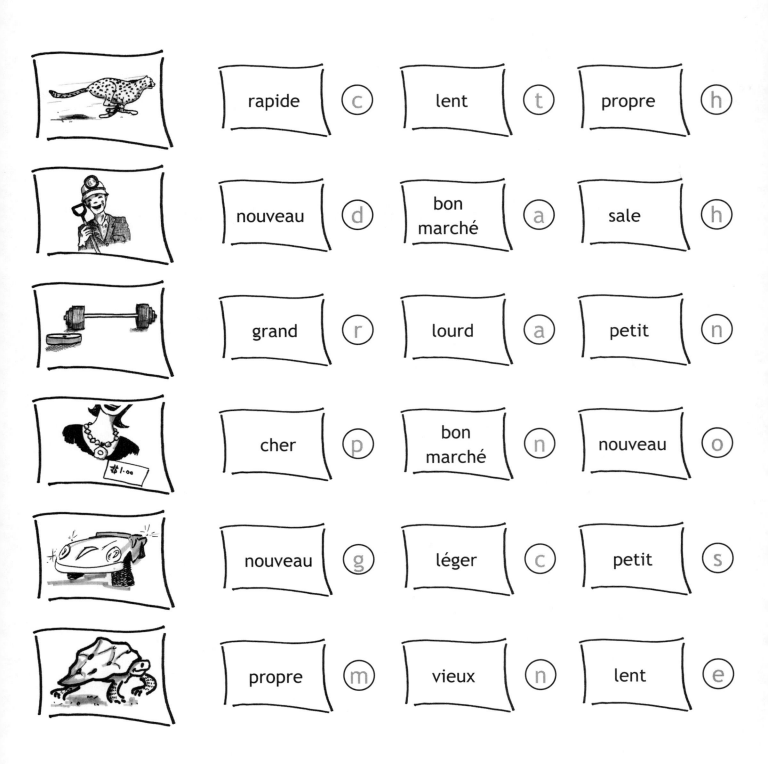

| | | | | | |
|---|---|---|---|---|---|
| rapide | ⓒ | lent | ⓣ | propre | ⓗ |
| nouveau | ⓓ | bon marché | ⓐ | sale | ⓗ |
| grand | ⓡ | lourd | ⓐ | petit | ⓝ |
| cher | ⓟ | bon marché | ⓝ | nouveau | ⓞ |
| nouveau | ⓖ | léger | ⓒ | petit | ⓢ |
| propre | ⓜ | vieux | ⓝ | lent | ⓔ |

**E**nglish word: ⓒ ◯ ◯ ◯ ◯ ◯

# Find the odd one out in these groups of words.

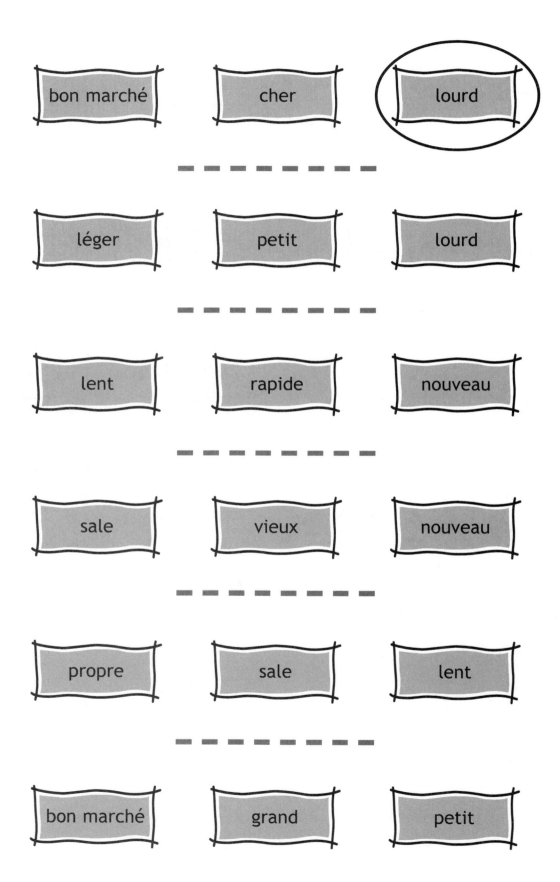

bon marché    cher    **lourd**

léger    petit    lourd

lent    rapide    nouveau

sale    vieux    nouveau

propre    sale    lent

bon marché    grand    petit

◎ **F**inally, join the English words to their French opposites, as in the example.

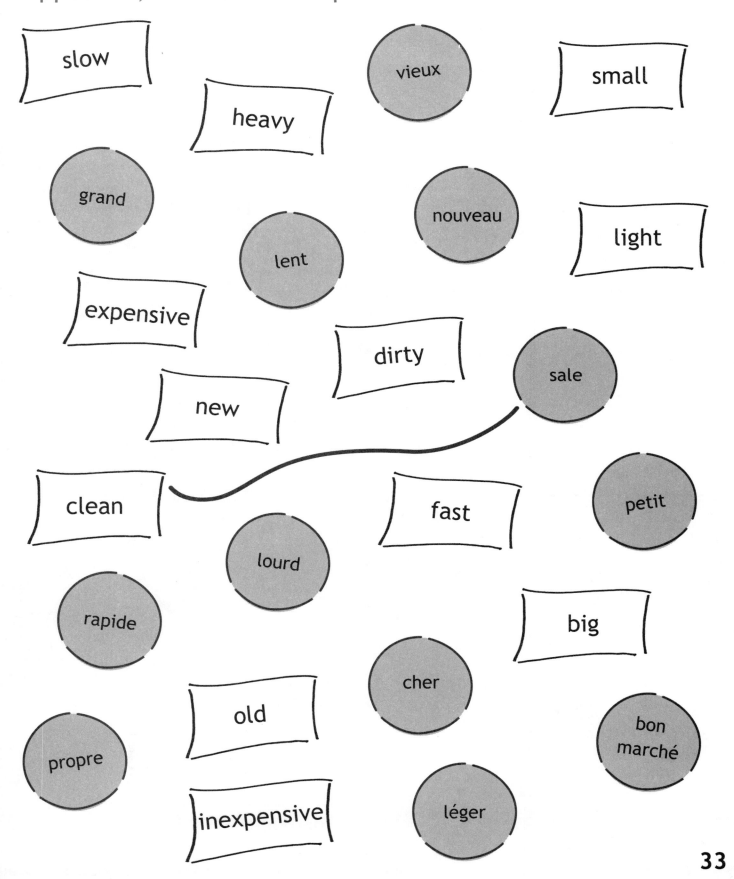

slow

vieux

small

heavy

grand

nouveau

light

lent

expensive

dirty

sale

new

clean

fast

petit

lourd

rapide

big

old

cher

bon marché

propre

inexpensive

léger

# 6 ANIMALS

Look at the pictures.
Tear out the flashcards for this topic.
Follow steps 1 and 2 of the plan in the introduction.

**le canard** *ler canar*

**l'âne**
*l'ahn*

**le chat**
*ler sha*

**le chien**
*ler shi-eñ*

**le lapin**
*ler lapeñ*

**le singe**
*ler señzh*

**le poisson** *ler pwassoñ*

**le mouton** *ler mootoñ*

**la souris** *la sooree*

**la vache** *la vash*

**le cheval**
*ler shev-al*

**le taureau**
*ler toroh*

Match the animals to their associated pictures, as in the example.

le lapin

le singe

le cheval

le chat

le mouton

la souris

le chien

la vache

le poisson

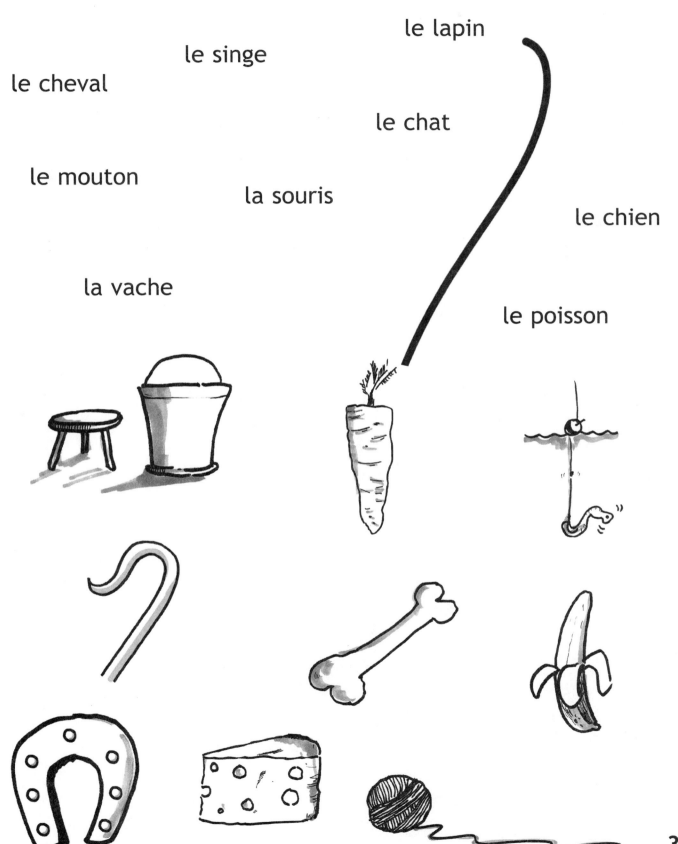

**S**omeone has ripped up the French words for animals. Can you join the two halves of the words, as the example?

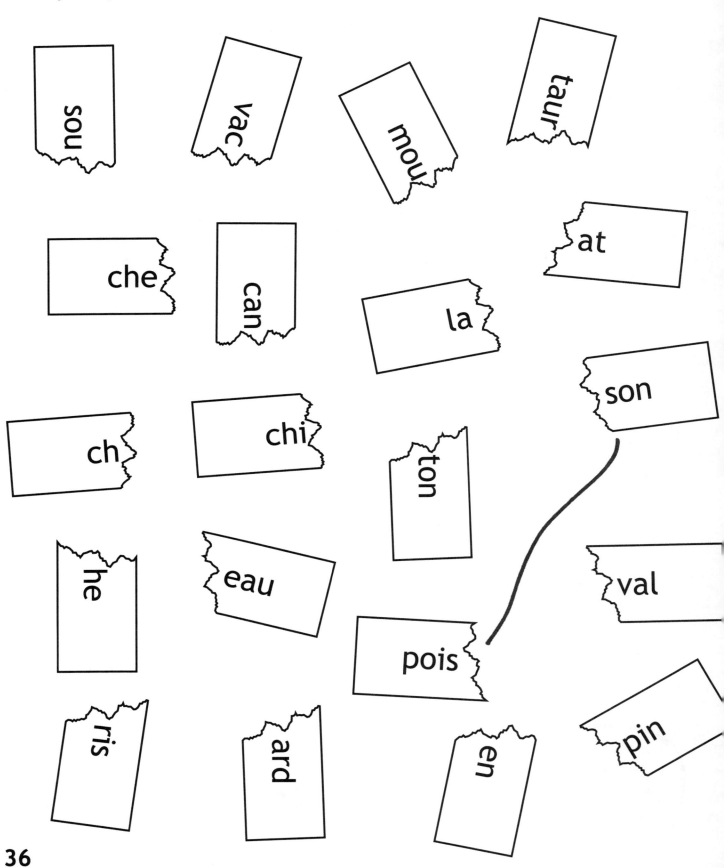

Check (✔) the animal words you can find in the word pile.

le lac

le chat

lent

la voiture

le lapin

l'âne

le mouton

le lit

lourd

le vélo

le magasin

la jupe

la colline

le taureau

la vache

le poisson

37

## Join the French animals to their English equivalents.

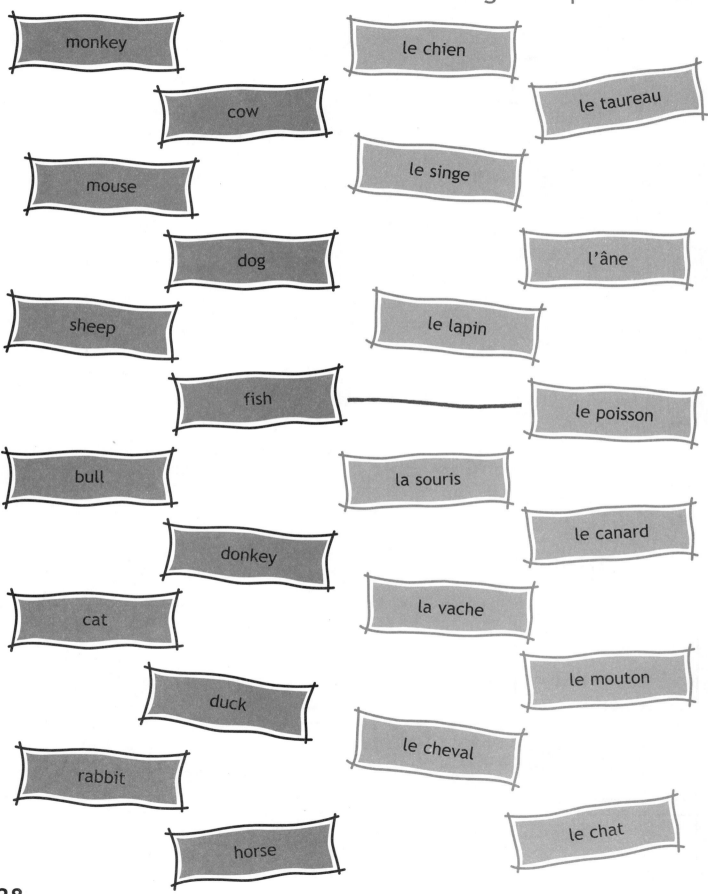

monkey

le chien

cow

le taureau

mouse

le singe

dog

l'âne

sheep

le lapin

fish — le poisson

bull

la souris

donkey

le canard

cat

la vache

duck

le mouton

rabbit

le cheval

horse

le chat

# ⑦ PARTS OF THE BODY

Look at the pictures of parts of the body.
Tear out the flashcards for this topic.
Follow steps 1 and 2 of the plan in the introduction.

**le doigt**
*ler dwa*

**la tête**
*la tet*

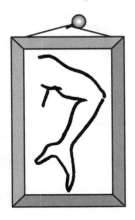

**le bras**
*ler bra*

**l'œil**  *l'oy*

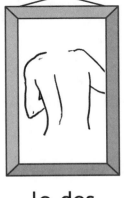

**le dos**
*ler doh*

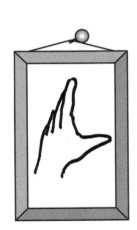

**la main**
*la meñ*

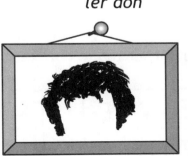

**les cheveux**  *lay shev-ur*

**la jambe**
*la zhomb*

**le ventre**
*ler voñtr*

**l'oreille**
*l'orayy*

**le nez**
*ler nay*

**la bouche**
*la boosh*

39

◎ **M**atch the pictures with the words, as in the example.

la tête

le ventre

le bras

l'œil

la main

les cheveux

le doigt

le dos

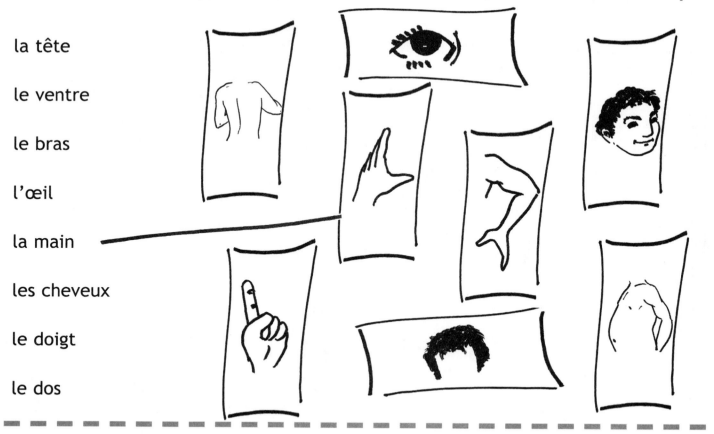

- - - - - - - - - - - - - - - - - - - - - - - - - - - - - - - - - - - - - - - - -

◎ **S**ee if you can find and circle six parts of the body in the word square, then draw them in the boxes below.
The words can run left to right, or top to bottom:

| S | C | H | E | V | E | U | X |
|---|---|---|---|---|---|---|---|
| I | C | U | Z | H | R | B | I |
| C | M | L | D | S | V | O | V |
| J | A | M | B | E | R | U | A |
| R | I | A | U | I | L | C | N |
| I | N | N | N | L | I | H | E |
| O | R | E | I | L | L | E | E |
| O | E | Z | P | R | T | A | T |

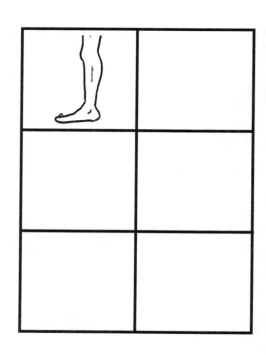

**40**

Write the words in the correct column, as in the example.

| le | la | l' | les |
|---|---|---|---|
| le nez | | | |

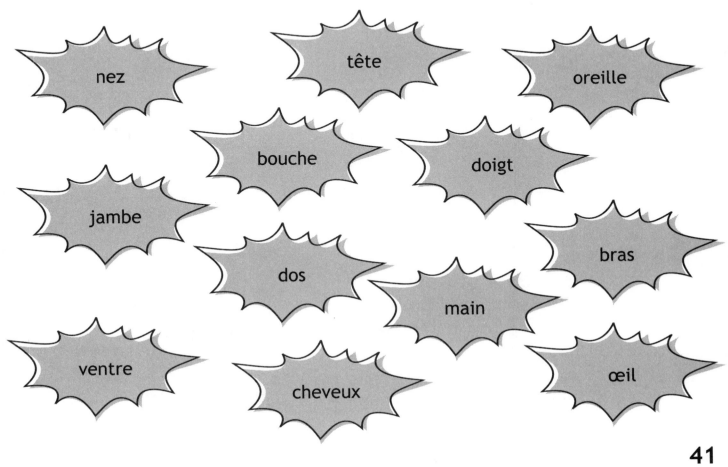

nez

tête

oreille

bouche

doigt

jambe

dos

bras

main

ventre

cheveux

œil

Label the body with the correct number, and write *le, la, l'* or *les* in front of the words.

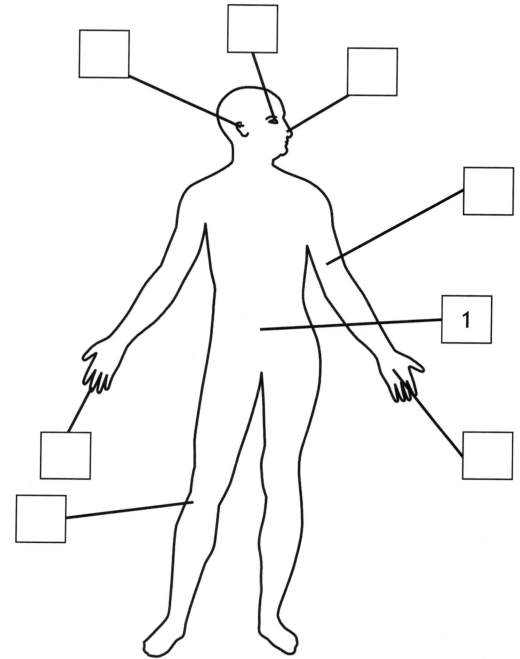

1 ___ ventre

2 ___ bras

3 ___ nez

4 ___ main

5 ___ oreille

6 ___ jambe

7 ___ œil

8 ___ doigt

Finally, match the French words, their pronunciation, and the English meanings, as in the example.

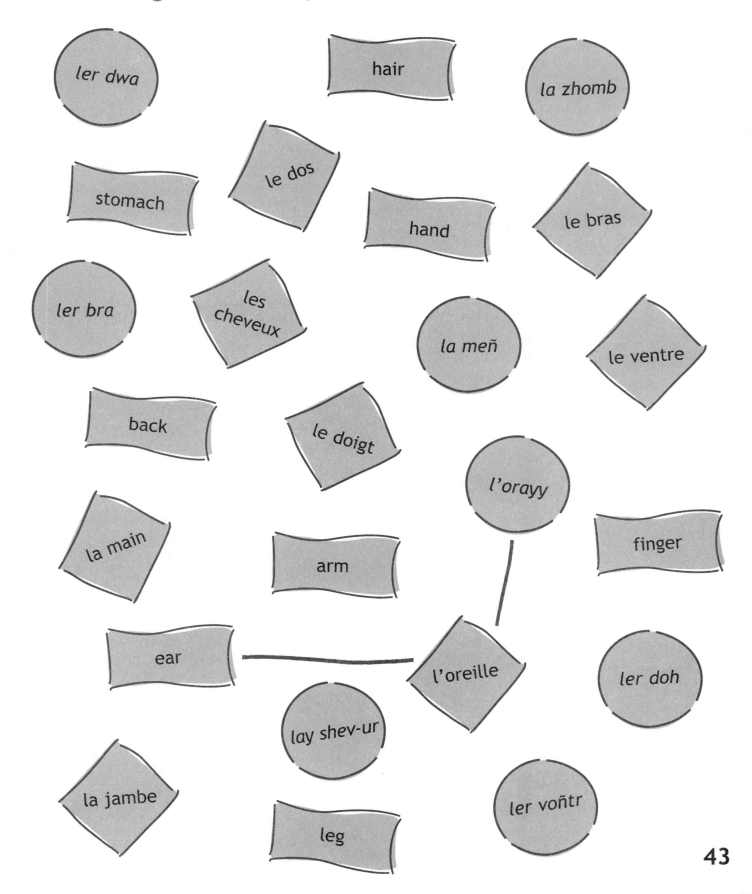

ler dwa

hair

la zhomb

le dos

stomach

hand

le bras

ler bra

les cheveux

la meñ

le ventre

back

le doigt

l'orayy

finger

la main

arm

ear

l'oreille

ler doh

lay shev-ur

la jambe

leg

ler voñtr

# ⑧ USEFUL EXPRESSIONS

Look at the pictures.
Tear out the flashcards for this topic.
Follow steps 1 and 2 of the plan in the introduction.

**où?** *oo*

**bonjour** *boñzhoor*

**au revoir**
*oh rewa-r*

---

**non**
*noñ*

**oui**
*wee*

**hier**
*ee-air*

**aujourd'hui**
*oh-zhoor-dwee*

**demain**
*demeñ*

---

**là** *la*

**maintenant**
*meñt-noñ*

**combien?**
*combyeñ*

**ici**
*eesee*

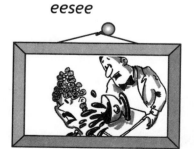

**s'il vous plaît**
*s'eelvoo-pleh*

**pardon** *pardoñ*

**chouette!**
*shooet*

**merci**
*mairsee*

## ◎ **M**atch the French words to their English equivalents.

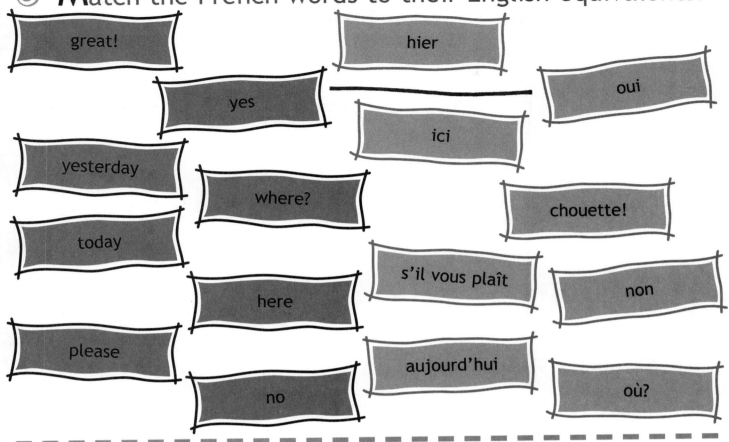

great! · hier · yes · oui · ici · yesterday · where? · chouette! · today · s'il vous plaît · non · here · please · aujourd'hui · où? · no

- - - - - - - - - - - - - - - - - - - - -

## ◎ **F**ill in the missing letters in these expressions.

c _ m b _ e _ ?

_ e r _ i

p _ r _ o _

_ o _ _ o u r

d e _ _ i _

a u _ o _ r d' _ _ _

_ u  r e _ o _ _

c _ o _ e _ _ e!

_ à

m _ _ n t _ n _ n t

Choose the French word that matches the picture to fill in the English word at the bottom of the page.

| Picture | | | |
|---|---|---|---|
| ☝️ doorbell | ici ⓟ | non ⓒ | oui ⓣ |
| waiter | merci ⓙ | pardon ⓐ | s'il vous plaît ⓛ |
| ✗ | oui Ⓜ | non ⓔ | aujourd'hui ⓘ |
| handshake | là ⓑ | bonjour ⓐ | s'il vous plaît ⓧ |
| soldier | où? ⓢ | combien? ⓗ | chouette! ⓣ |
| ✔ | bonjour ⓑ | non ⓨ | oui ⓔ |

English word:  ⓟ ◯ ◯ ◯ ◯ ◯

What are these people saying? Write the correct number in each speech bubble, as in the example.

1 bonjour    2 s'il vous plaît    3 oui    4 non

5 ici    6 pardon    7 où?    8 combien?

◎ **F**inally, match the French words, their pronunciation, and the English meanings, as in the example.

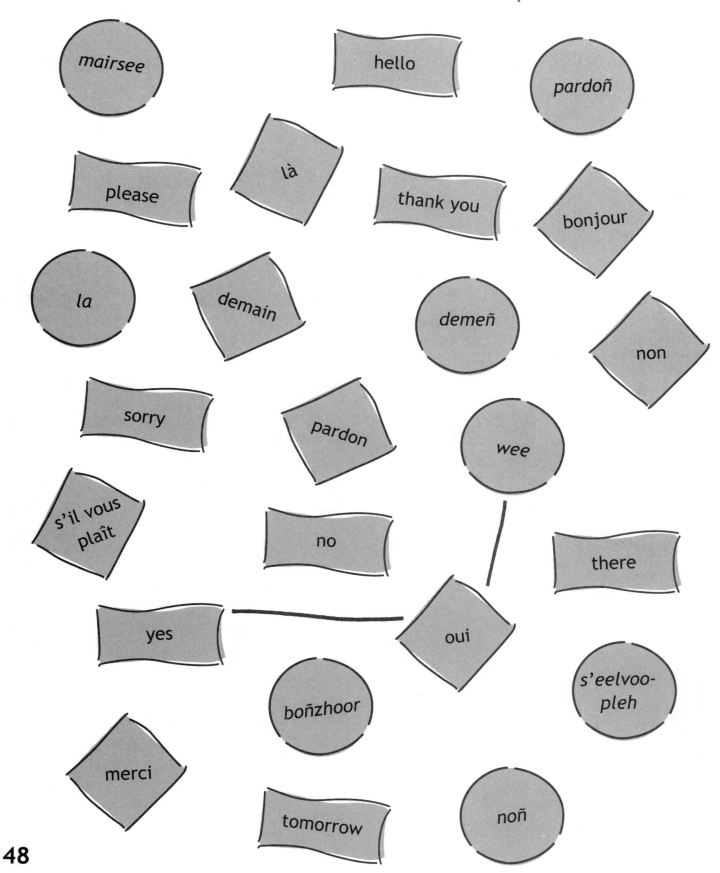

mairsee

hello

pardoñ

là

please

thank you

bonjour

la

demain

demeñ

non

sorry

pardon

wee

s'il vous plaît

no

there

yes

oui

s'eelvoo-pleh

boñzhoor

merci

tomorrow

noñ

48

# ● ROUND-UP

This section is designed to review all the 100 words you have met in the different topics. It is a good idea to test yourself with your flashcards before trying this section.

- - - - - - - - - - - - - - - - - - - - - - - -

◎ The ten objects below are all in the picture. Can you find and circle them?

la porte     la fleur     le lit     le manteau     le chapeau

le vélo     la chaise     le chien     le poisson     la chaussette

See if you can remember all these words.

aujourd'hui

la boulangerie

rapide

le nez

la pluie

oui

le placard

le taureau

la robe

bon marché

la rivière

la jambe

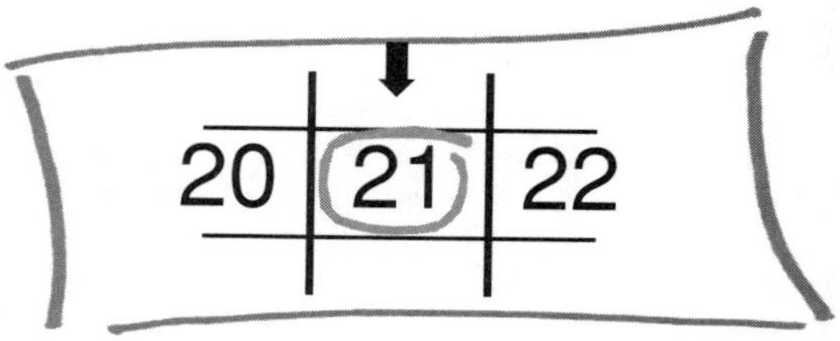

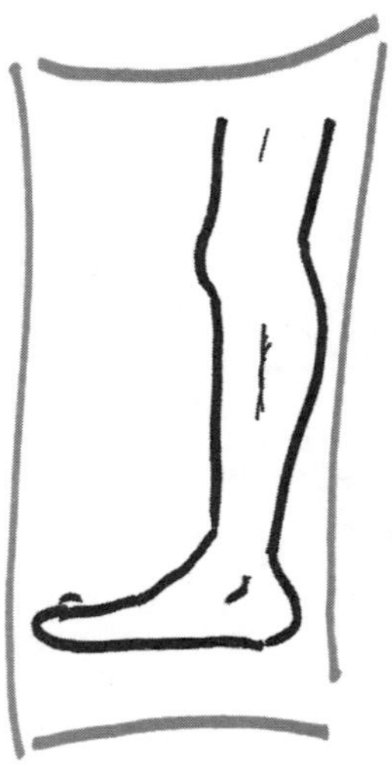

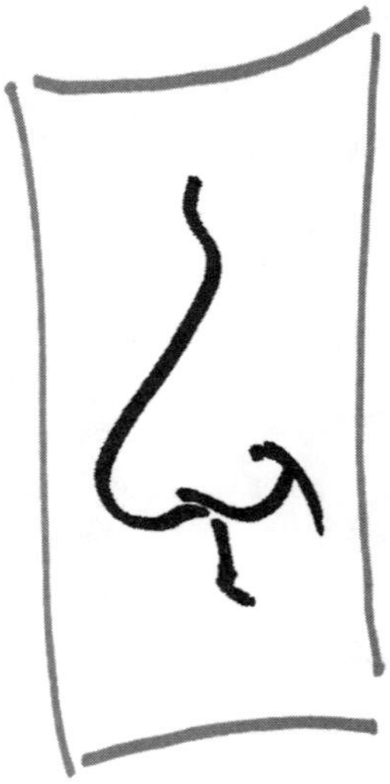

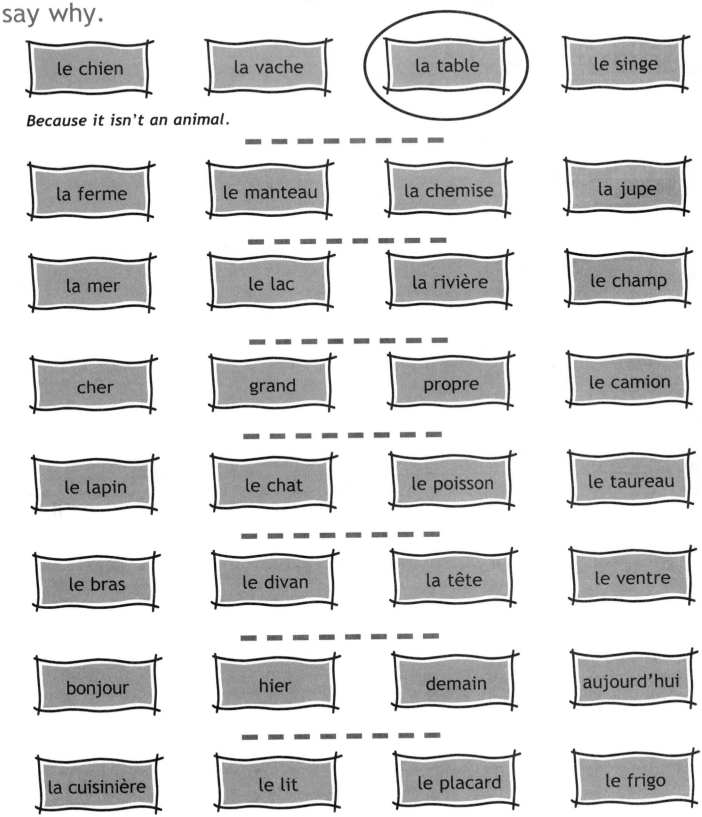

◎ **F**ind the odd one out in these groups of words and say why.

| le chien | la vache | la table | le singe |

*Because it isn't an animal.*

| la ferme | le manteau | la chemise | la jupe |

| la mer | le lac | la rivière | le champ |

| cher | grand | propre | le camion |

| le lapin | le chat | le poisson | le taureau |

| le bras | le divan | la tête | le ventre |

| bonjour | hier | demain | aujourd'hui |

| la cuisinière | le lit | le placard | le frigo |

◎ **L**ook at the objects below for 30 seconds.

◎ **C**over the picture and try to remember all the objects.
Circle the French words for those objects you remember.

la fleur

la chaussure

merci

la porte

la voiture

non

ici

le manteau

le camion

la ceinture

la montagne

la chaise

le cheval

le chapeau

la chaussette

la cravate

l'œil

le lit

l'écharpe

le banc

le tapis

le singe

Now match the French words, their pronunciation, and the English meanings, as in the example.

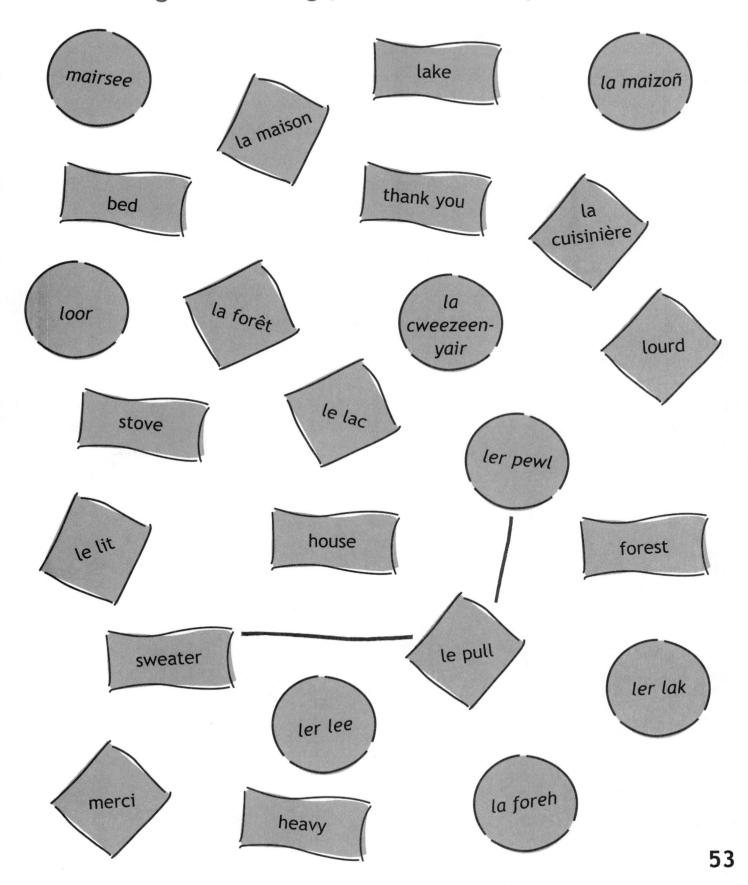

mairsee

lake

la maizoñ

la maison

bed

thank you

la cuisinière

loor

la forêt

la cweezeen-yair

lourd

stove

le lac

ler pewl

le lit

house

forest

sweater

le pull

ler lak

ler lee

merci

heavy

la foreh

| le divan (w) | le banc (g) | l'oreille (t) |
| le manteau (o) | le lac (a) | le pont (e) |
| où? (m) | combien? (l) | demain (i) |
| la vache (b) | la fenêtre (l) | la boucherie (h) |
| la maison (e) | la bouche (a) | le chien (d) |
| l'œil (o) | l'oreille (p) | la souris (v) |
| la colline (n) | la ferme (y) | le manteau (r) |
| le lapin (n) | la rue (e) | la chaise (s) |

54  **E**nglish phrase: 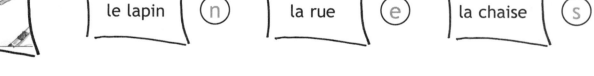 (w) ◯ ◯ ◯   ◯ ◯ ◯ ◯ !

Look at the two pictures and check (✔) the objects that are different in Picture B.

Picture A

la jupe ☐

le pantalon ☐

la porte ☐

le chat ☐

la chaise ☐

le poisson ☐

la chaussette ☐

le chien ☐

Picture B

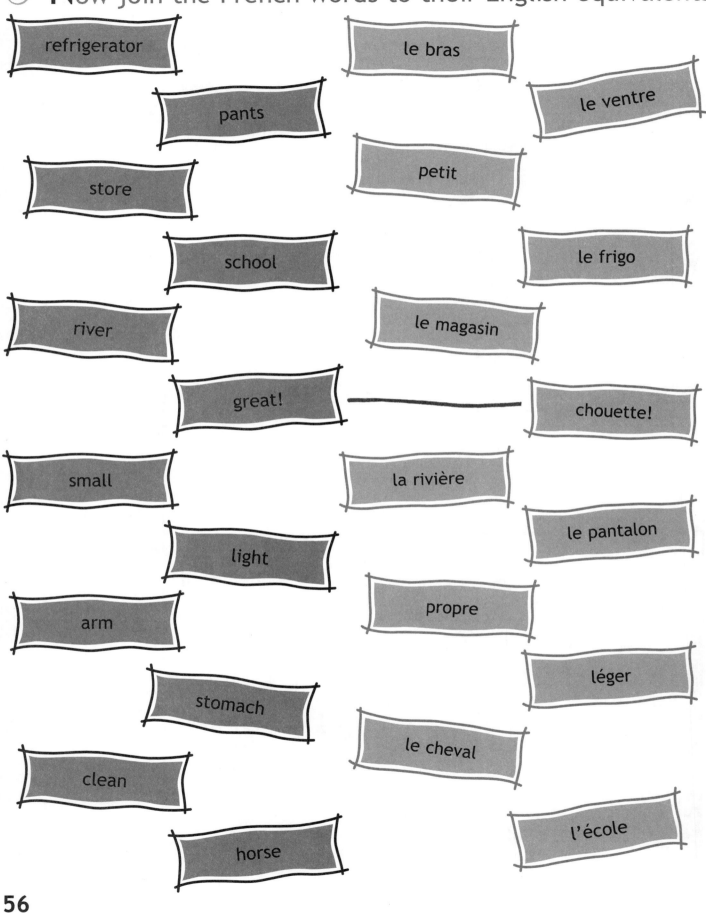

refrigerator

le bras

pants

le ventre

store

petit

school

le frigo

river

le magasin

great! ———— chouette!

small

la rivière

light

le pantalon

arm

propre

stomach

léger

clean

le cheval

horse

l'école

# Complete the crossword using the picture clues.

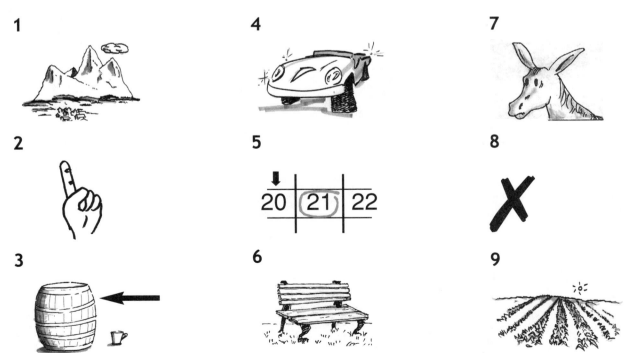

**1**

**2**

**3**

**4**

**5**

**6**

**7**

**8**

**9**

# ◎ Snake game.

● You will need a die and counter(s). You can challenge yourself to reach the finish or play with someone else. You have to throw the exact number to finish.

● Throw the die and move forward that number of spaces. When you land on a word you must pronounce it (with **le**, **la**, **l'** or **les** if appropriate) and say what it means in English. If you can't, you have to go back to the square you came from.

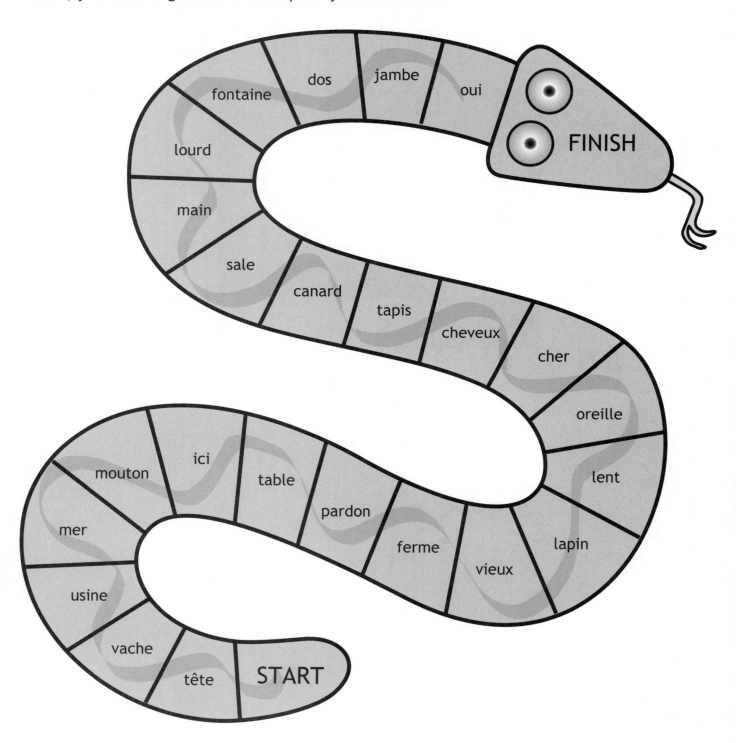

# Answers

## 1 Around the home

**Page 10 (top)**

See page 9 for correct picture.

**Page 10 (bottom)**

| | |
|---|---|
| door | la porte |
| cupboard | le placard |
| stove | la cuisinière |
| bed | le lit |
| table | la table |
| chair | la chaise |
| refrigerator | le frigo |
| computer | l'ordinateur |

**Page 11 (top)**

| | |
|---|---|
| chaise | divan |
| frigo | placard |
| fenêtre | table |
| cuisinière | tapis |
| porte | étagère |

**Page 11 (bottom)**

| | | | | | | | |
|---|---|---|---|---|---|---|---|
| B | A | T | A | P | I | S | D |
| I | C | U | H | O | R | A | I |
| C | H | L | D | R | V | A | V |
| F | E | N | Ê | T | R | E | A |
| R | L | A | U | F | L | A | N |
| I | R | C | H | A | I | S | E |
| G | D | I | V | A | T | O | E |
| O | E | P | O | R | T | A | T |

**Page 12**

**Page 13**

English word: window

## 2 Clothes

**Page 15 (top)**

| | |
|---|---|
| la robe | le pull |
| le chapeau | la ceinture |
| la chemise | la cravate |
| l'écharpe | la jupe |

**Page 15 (bottom)**

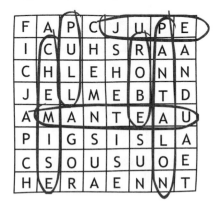

| | | | | | | | |
|---|---|---|---|---|---|---|---|
| F | A | P | C | J | U | P | E |
| I | C | U | H | S | R | A | A |
| C | H | L | E | H | O | N | N |
| J | E | L | M | E | B | T | D |
| A | M | A | N | T | E | A | U |
| P | I | G | S | I | S | L | A |
| C | S | O | U | S | U | O | E |
| H | E | R | A | E | N | N | T |

**Page 16**

| | | |
|---|---|---|
| hat | le chapeau | *ler shapoh* |
| shoe | la chaussure | *la shoh-sewr* |
| sock | la chaussette | *la shoh-set* |
| scarf | l'écharpe | *l'aysharp* |
| tie | la cravate | *la kravat* |
| belt | la ceinture | *la señtewr* |
| coat | le manteau | *ler moñtoh* |
| pants | le pantalon | *ler poñtaloñ* |

**Page 17**

| | |
|---|---|
| chapeau (hat) | 1 |
| manteau (coat) | 0 |
| ceinture (belt) | 2 |
| chaussure (shoe) | 2 (1 pair) |
| pantalon (pants) | 1 |
| écharpe (scarf) | 1 |
| robe (dress) | 0 |
| chaussette (sock) | 6 (3 pairs) |
| jupe (skirt) | 0 |
| cravate (tie) | 2 |
| chemise (shirt) | 4 |
| pull (sweater) | 1 |

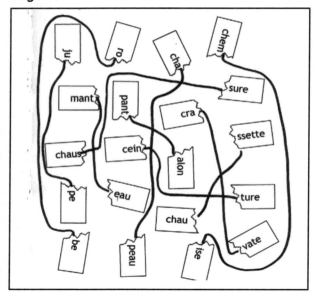

English word: school

**Page 23**

| le | la | l' |
| --- | --- | --- |
| le banc | la boulangerie | l'usine |
| le camion | la maison | l'école |
| le vélo | la voiture | |
| le magasin | la fontaine | |
| | la rue | |
| | la boucherie | |

## ❸ AROUND TOWN

**Page 20 (top)**

| truck | le camion |
| --- | --- |
| store | le magasin |
| factory | l'usine |
| bench | le banc |
| car | la voiture |
| fountain | la fontaine |
| school | l'école |
| house | la maison |

**Page 20 (bottom)**

| bicycle | 4 |
| --- | --- |
| bench | 7 |
| house | 2 |
| fountain | 6 |
| truck | 1 |
| road | 3 |
| car | 5 |

**Page 21**

1 le banc
2 la voiture
3 la fontaine
4 l'usine
5 le camion
6 l'école
7 la rue
8 la boucherie
9 la boulangerie

## ❹ COUNTRYSIDE

**Page 25**

See page 24 for correct picture.

**Page 26**

| pont | ✔ | champ | ✔ |
| --- | --- | --- | --- |
| arbre | ✔ | forêt | ✔ |
| pluie | ✘ | lac | ✘ |
| colline | ✘ | rivière | ✔ |
| montagne | ✔ | fleur | ✔ |
| mer | ✘ | ferme | ✘ |

**Page 27 (top)**

| la pluie | la fleur |
| --- | --- |
| la forêt | la rivière |
| l'arbre | le lac |
| la mer | la colline |

**Page 27 (bottom)**

**Page 28**

| | | |
|---|---|---|
| sea | la mer | *la mair* |
| lake | le lac | *ler lak* |
| rain | la pluie | *la plwee* |
| farm | la ferme | *la fairm* |
| flower | la fleur | *la flur* |
| mountain | la montagne | *la moñtanye* |
| river | la rivière | *la reeveeyair* |
| field | le champ | *ler shoñ* |

## 5 OPPOSITES

**Page 30**

| | |
|---|---|
| expensive | cher |
| big | grand |
| light | léger |
| slow | lent |
| clean | propre |
| inexpensive | bon marché |
| dirty | sale |
| small | petit |
| heavy | lourd |
| new | nouveau |
| fast | rapide |
| old | vieux |

**Page 31**
English word: change

**Page 32**
Odd one outs are those which are not opposites:
lourd
petit
nouveau
sale
lent
bon marché

**Page 33**

| | |
|---|---|
| old | nouveau |
| big | petit |
| new | vieux |
| slow | rapide |
| dirty | propre |

| | |
|---|---|
| small | grand |
| heavy | léger |
| clean | sale |
| light | lourd |
| expensive | bon marché |
| inexpensive | cher |
| fast | lent |

## 6 ANIMALS

**Page 35**

la vache    le lapin    le poisson

le mouton    le chien    le singe

le cheval    la souris    le chat

**Page 36**

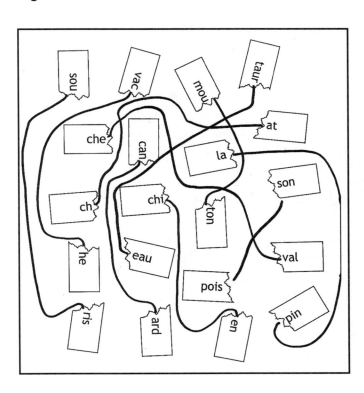

**Page 37**

| | | | | |
|---|---|---|---|---|
| donkey | ✔ | mouse | ✘ |
| monkey | ✘ | cat | ✔ |
| sheep | ✔ | dog | ✘ |
| bull | ✔ | cow | ✔ |
| fish | ✔ | horse | ✘ |
| duck | ✘ | rabbit | ✔ |

**Page 38**

| | |
|---|---|
| monkey | le singe |
| cow | la vache |
| mouse | la souris |
| dog | le chien |
| sheep | le mouton |
| fish | le poisson |
| bull | le taureau |
| donkey | l'âne |
| cat | le chat |
| duck | le canard |
| rabbit | le lapin |
| horse | le cheval |

# ❼ PARTS OF THE BODY

**Page 40 (top)**

See page 39 for correct picture.

**Page 40 (bottom)**

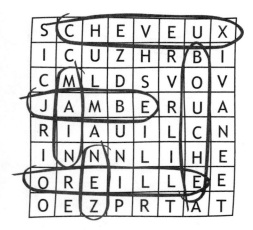

You should have also drawn pictures of:
leg; mouth; ear; nose; hand; hair

**Page 41**

| le | la | l' | les |
|---|---|---|---|
| le nez | la tête | l'œil | les cheveux |
| le bras | la main | l'oreille | |
| le doigt | la jambe | | |
| le ventre | la bouche | | |
| le dos | | | |

**Page 42**

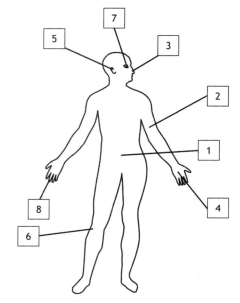

| | | | |
|---|---|---|---|
| 1 | le ventre | 2 | le bras |
| 3 | le nez | 4 | la main |
| 5 | l'oreille | 6 | la jambe |
| 7 | l'œil | 8 | le doigt |

**Page 43**

| | | |
|---|---|---|
| ear | l'oreille | l'orayy |
| hair | les cheveux | lay shev-ur |
| hand | la main | la meñ |
| stomach | le ventre | ler voñtr |
| arm | le bras | ler bra |
| back | le dos | ler doh |
| finger | le doigt | ler dwa |
| leg | la jambe | la zhomb |

## 8 Useful expressions

**Page 45 (top)**

| | |
|---|---|
| great! | chouette! |
| yes | oui |
| yesterday | hier |
| where? | où? |
| today | aujourd'hui |
| here | ici |
| please | s'il vous plaît |
| no | non |

**Page 45 (bottom)**

| | |
|---|---|
| combien? | aujourd'hui |
| merci | au revoir |
| pardon | chouette! |
| bonjour | là |
| demain | maintenant |

**Page 46**

English word: please

**Page 47**

**Page 48**

| | | |
|---|---|---|
| yes | oui | *wee* |
| hello | bonjour | *boñzhoor* |
| no | non | *noñ* |
| sorry | pardon | *pardoñ* |
| please | s'il vous plaît | *s'eelvoo-pleh* |
| there | là | *la* |
| thank you | merci | *mairsee* |
| tomorrow | demain | *demeñ* |

## Round-up

**Page 49**

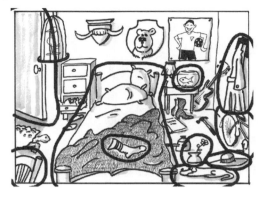

**Page 50**

= la pluie

= le taureau

= oui

= le placard

= bon marché

= aujourd'hui

= la rivière

= le nez

= la robe

= la jambe

= rapide

= la boulangerie

**Page 51**

la table (Because it isn't an animal.)

la ferme (Because it isn't an item of clothing.)

le champ (Because it isn't connected with water.)

le camion (Because it isn't a descriptive word.)

le poisson (Because it lives in water/doesn't have legs.)

le divan (Because it isn't a part of the body.)

bonjour (Because it isn't an expression of time.)

le lit (Because you wouldn't find it in the kitchen.)

## Page 52

Words that appear in the picture:

la cravate

la voiture

la fleur

la chaussure

le chapeau

le camion

le singe

le tapis

la chaise

la ceinture

l'écharpe

## Page 53

| | | |
|---|---|---|
| sweater | le pull | *ler pewl* |
| lake | le lac | *ler lak* |
| thank you | merci | *mairsee* |
| bed | le lit | *ler lee* |
| house | la maison | *la maizoñ* |
| forest | la forêt | *la foreh* |
| stove | la cuisinière | *la cweezeen-yair* |
| heavy | lourd | *loor* |

## Page 54

English phrase: well done!

## Page 55

| | |
|---|---|
| la jupe | ✗ |
| le pantalon | ✔ (shade) |
| la porte | ✔ (handle) |
| le chat | ✗ |
| la chaise | ✔ (back) |
| le poisson | ✔ (direction) |
| la chaussette | ✔ (pattern) |
| le chien | ✗ |

## Page 56

| | |
|---|---|
| refrigerator | le frigo |
| pants | le pantalon |
| store | le magasin |
| school | l'école |
| river | la rivière |
| great! | chouette! |
| small | petit |
| light | léger |
| arm | le bras |
| stomach | le ventre |
| clean | propre |
| horse | le cheval |

## Page 57

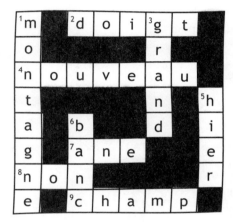

## Page 58

Here are the English equivalents of the word, in order from START to FINISH:

| | | | |
|---|---|---|---|
| head | la tête | ear | l'oreille |
| cow | la vache | expensive | cher |
| factory | l'usine | hair | les cheveux |
| sea | la mer | rug | le tapis |
| sheep | le mouton | duck | le canard |
| here | ici | dirty | sale |
| table | la table | hand | la main |
| sorry | pardon | heavy | lourd |
| farm | la ferme | fountain | la fontaine |
| old | vieux | back | le dos |
| rabbit | le lapin | leg | la jambe |
| slow | lent | yes | oui |

l'ordinateur

la fenêtre

la table

le placard

le frigo

la chaise

le divan

la cuisinière

la porte

le lit

l'étagère

le tapis

| window | computer |
| --- | --- |
| cupboard | table |
| chair | refrigerator |
| stove | sofa |
| bed | door |
| rug | shelf |

| | |
|---|---|
| la ceinture | le manteau |
| la jupe | le chapeau |
| la cravate | la chaussure |
| le pull | la chemise |
| l'écharpe | la chaussette |
| le pantalon | la robe |

| | |
|---|---|
| coat | belt |
| hat | skirt |
| shoe | tie |
| shirt | sweater |
| sock | scarf |
| dress | pants |

l'école

la voiture

la rue

le camion

l'usine

le magasin

le banc

le vélo

la boucherie

la boulangerie

la fontaine

la maison

car

school

truck

road

store

factory

bicycle

bench

baker

butcher

house

fountain

le lac

la forêt

la colline

la mer

la montagne

l'arbre

la pluie

la fleur

le pont

la rivière

la ferme

le champ

| forest | lake |
| --- | --- |
| sea | hill |
| tree | mountain |
| flower | rain |
| river | bridge |
| field | farm |

| | |
|---|---|
| lourd | léger |
| grand | petit |
| vieux | nouveau |
| rapide | lent |
| propre | sale |
| bon marché | cher |

| | |
|---|---|
| light | heavy |
| small | big |
| new | old |
| slow | fast |
| dirty | clean |
| expensive | inexpensive |

| le canard | le chat |
| --- | --- |
| la souris | la vache |
| le lapin | le chien |
| le cheval | le singe |
| le taureau | le poisson |
| l'âne | le mouton |

| | |
|---|---|
| cat | duck |
| cow | mouse |
| dog | rabbit |
| monkey | horse |
| fish | bull |
| sheep | donkey |

| le bras | le doigt |
| --- | --- |
| la tête | la bouche |
| l'oreille | la jambe |
| la main | le ventre |
| l'œil | les cheveux |
| le nez | le dos |

finger

arm

mouth

head

leg

ear

stomach

hand

hair

eye

back

nose

| | |
|---|---|
| s'il vous plaît | merci |
| oui | non |
| bonjour | au revoir |
| hier | aujourd'hui |
| demain | où? |
| ici | là |
| pardon | combien? |
| chouette! | maintenant |

| | |
|---|---|
| thank you | please |
| no | yes |
| goodbye | hello |
| today | yesterday |
| where? | tomorrow |
| there | here |
| how much? | sorry! |
| now | great! |